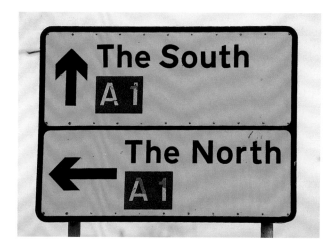

A1

JON **NICHOLSON**

HarperCollins*Illustrated*

Introduction by
Nigel Richardson

It has yet to be eulogised in rock'n'roll songs or seminal novels, as has Route 66 in the USA. But, in its piecemeal and self-effacing way, our own A1 tells a unique story about Britain and how we see ourselves. As with a great river, the four-hundred-mile route from London to Edinburgh has its own lore and landscape. The fattest man in English history died on the road: Daniel Lambert weighed nearly fifty-three stones when he pegged out in the Wagon and Horses in Stamford in 1809. In 1925, three years after the old Great North Road received the cipher A1, Margaret Thatcher was born above the family grocer's shop that fronted the road in Grantham. And thirty years ago, as I made my way to school, the driver of a speeding Ford Zodiac almost spread me across the broken white lines that marked the road between Doncaster and Bawtry.

That close shave bred in me an initial fear of the A1 that modified into respect, and then fascination, as I grew up. The more I have driven the road between London and South Yorkshire, and often beyond, the greater the feel I have developed for the gradations of history and topography that inform its character. When I saw Jon Nicholson's photographs, I realised we shared a vision of the A1.

Nicholson had already completed a major photographic record of Route 66, that most iconic of highways that, in the words of the song, 'winds from Chicago to LA, more than two thousand miles all the way.' The A1 may be a more modest affair, but the challenge, photographically, was just as stiff. 'A lot of the work I do is in the US,' he says. 'I may end up travelling eight hundred miles between photographs. It's easy to be motivated and focused. Here, if it's raining, the temptation is to go home and try again the next day.' His intention with these pictures was 'to see the familiar with a fresh eye; to reminisce, while acknowledging the march of progress.' The maddening punctuation of contraflow systems, the Northumbrian hills sprinkled with snow, the submarine light of truckers' cafés – through such images his unflinching lens succeeds in distilling the strange beauty of the road that Dorothy L Sayers dismissed as 'a long, flat, steel-grey ribbon'.

According to the old coaching timetables, that ribbon starts just north of Smithfield Market, in the heart of medieval London, though a later starting point, the one favoured by Jon Nicholson in this book, is the old General Post Office at St Martin's Le Grand by St Paul's Cathedral. It climbs clear of the capital in a series of giant steps – Islington, Highgate, Mill Hill – levels out through the lush pastureland of Hertfordshire and the market gardens of Bedfordshire, skirts the Wash where the light lends the air a soft, slightly unfocused quality, and unravels through an East Midlands of electricity pylons and red-brick farmsteads. Where the road crosses the Tyne in Newcastle, the riverscape is part Canaletto, part LS Lowry. Through the unspoilt tracts of the Borders and East Lothian, if you're lucky, the light will shine dazzlingly on the ocean that rushes to lap at the southbound verges.

For a road with a reputation – south of Newcastle, at least – for unutterable flatness, it features several astonishing perpendicular features. The first, assuming a northbound route, is Ferrybridge power station in West Yorkshire, belching Himalayas of smoke above Castleford and Pontefract; Antony Gormley's gigantic steel sculpture, Angel of the North, bestows benediction with outstretched wings on travellers through Gateshead, while Holy Island and its Priory of Lindisfarne rise like Camelot from Northumberland's coastal frets.

Then there are the irresistible place names sprinkled like stardust on road signs along the route: Water Newton and Burton Coggles, Honey Pot Lane and Pity Me, Conundrum and Phantassie.

This is the broad sweep, but the precise route has chopped and changed down the years. The stretch of road on which I almost became a statistic had been reclassified the A638 because the A1 bypassed Doncaster, as it does almost all the towns and villages that once stood on its route. In this sense the road has been organic, adapting to the changing demands and volume of traffic to create the present amalgam of Roman road, medieval track, turnpike, coach road, dual carriageway and motorway. Unlike a modern, custom-built motorway the A1 has a sinuosity; it twists and turns, it keeps drivers on their toes, shedding now an inside and now an outside lane; and trees, not concrete, fringe its verges.

At least this remains the case on the three hundred-plus miles of road that have yet to be upgraded to motorway. In 1990, plans were announced to turn the entire road from London to Tyneside into motorway by the end of the millennium. Six years later these plans were withdrawn with just one new scheme — the Alconbury-Peterborough stretch — underway. For those of nostalgic bent this is good news as it preserves, for now, the A1's unique character. Nevertheless, the road will slowly succumb to improvements and homogenisation and as it does so the truckstops and lay-by cafés that advertise themselves with umbrellas and flags, the strawberry sellers and impromptu florists (I recently saw this sign near Sandy: 'Flowers three bunches a fivver (sic) next lay-by') that exist precisely because of the road's ad hoc provenance, will be erased one by one.

Take Kate's Cabin near Peterborough, where Nicholson's lens caught the lonely life of the trucker. Nowadays the name has been streamlined to KC's Diner, but a Kate's Cabin of one sort or another has stood on this site since 1800, when the original Kate built her original cabin. Nowadays 'Kate' is a jolly woman called Maria Arias, whose family has run KC's since the late 1980s. 'It's one of the oldest cafés in England,' she says. 'All the truckers know it. We provide the sort of food they can't get anywhere any more except at home, such as typical liver and onions. It's a friendly place and people feel happy here. What will they do when this goes?'

When institutions such as Kate's Cabin finally suffer death by concrete escarpment, important bits of the A1's history will certainly die with them. But those loops that have been fortuitously preserved by being severed from the main artery will continue to tell a story. I first realised this when, in childhood, I learned that beneath the extraordinarily wide grass verge bordering the road near our house were the remains of a Roman road. Where I trudged to school and finned Fords ignored the speed limit, legionnaires had marched through Yorkshire winters, no doubt dreaming of Rome. While a student I discovered in a second-hand bookshop a pocket-sized book bound in faded red cloth that sealed my fascination.

That book was *Great North Road* by Charles Harper, first published in 1901 in two volumes (London-York and York-Edinburgh). Harper wrote it after steam trains had superseded coaches and horses but before the advent of the car, when everyone assumed the railway, as Harper put it, 'had written Finis to the last chapter in the romantic story of the Great North Road'. It is an affectionate, elegiac portrait of a highway dappled by the shadows of overhanging trees and measured by weathered old milestones. Jon Nicholson has captured the most impressive of the road's old stone markers, the pillar surmounted by a globe that stands on Alconbury Hill, and his pictures of the May Day pageant at Ickwell Green near Sandy conjure an England in tune with Harper's nostalgic vision.

It was through the Harper book that I discovered the existence of an ancient variant of the route through north Nottinghamshire and decided, one fine spring morning, to find and drive it. In the road atlas this old highway was so minor it bore no road number. On the ground, it was little more than a farm track. The clue to its former status lay half-buried in a hedge on the north side of Gamston airport near Retford — a milestone which reads: 'From London 142 miles. Coach Road'. A mile north, I came across an old painted Romany caravan parked among the cow parsley on the verge; next to it a man with the looks of DH Lawrence tended a cooking pot over an open fire. This scene, which could have been one of the delicate line drawings in Harper's book come to life, is certainly the most extraordinary I have come across on the road. Another atmospheric capsule, frozen in time by the re-routing of the road, is the hamlet of Water Newton in Cambridgeshire: a handful of stone-built houses, a mouldering church with a stone Roman coffin lying casually in the churchyard, and never a soul about when I have visited.

On Jon Nicholson's first working journey up the A1 he photographed a fisherman and his son in Berwick upon Tweed. When they told him the old stage coaches used to have to ford the river, Nicholson realised just how primitive old-style travel must have been. To try to capture this rough-and-ready sense he mounted a camera outside the car as he drove the ford himself, and subsequently repeated this

technique on other stretches of road. But in this age of the fast car and
bullocking juggernaut it is impossible entirely to imagine what.the journey
between London and Edinburgh once entailed, either for passengers or freight.
Cocooned in our brushed-cotton cockpits, we travel at formerly unimaginable levels
of comfort and speed. If I put my foot down, and contraflows permitting, I can
drive the 160 miles from my flat in south-west London to my mother's home just
south of Doncaster in three and a half hours. In the late seventeenth century,
when the first official stage coach services were introduced, this journey took
four days and was more rightly a voyage of danger and discovery.

The land was unenclosed and traffic often avoided the treacherous ruts and bogs
of the most direct route by striking out across the fields. Though the road
retains a certain meandering quality, the most extreme kinks have been ironed out
over the years, with one striking exception — the crossing of the confluence of
the Great Ouse and Ivel rivers between Sandy in Bedfordshire and Eaton Socon in
Cambridgeshire. Here, incredibly, while the southbound carriageway crosses on a
modern steel bridge, the northern carriageway still uses the old stone bridge.
To reach it, the road takes the sharpest of all the turns on the A1, a left swing
so acute that the entire curve is zippered with black and white warning chevrons.

Throughout the eighteenth century delays and accidents were commonplace on the
journey north. Nicholas Nickelby, in Dickens's novel, is flung into the road
between Grantham and Newark when his stage coach flips over. The threat from
highwaymen was also a real one. Daniel Defoe, in *A Tour Through the Whole Island
of Great Britain*, written in 1724, notes that a treacherous dip known as Stangate
Hole, just north of Alconbury, is 'famous for being the most noted robbing-place

in all this part of the country'. Now it is part of the relatively new motorway section that runs from Alconbury to Peterborough (the old road, incidentally, immediately to the east, has been reclassified the B1043; several feet below its layers of tar and hardcore lies the Roman Ermine Street). But matters gradually improved, thanks to the imposition of road tolls and the evolution of road building techniques. By the 1830s, the golden era of the mail and stage coach, the journey time to Doncaster was sixteen or seventeen hours.

To maintain this average of 10 mph, horses had to be changed regularly and passengers fed and watered, which is where the coaching inns and posting houses came in. These quaint, venerable old structures were a favourite subject of nineteenth-century prints and came to epitomise the rose-tinted view of the old coaching days that prevailed in late Victorian times. Their subsequent fate has come to symbolise the evolution of the road. Who knows, now, the fantastically rambling, ivy-clad Bell at Barnby Moor in Nottinghamshire, which has lain off the A1 route for many years? Yet this was once the largest posting house in the north of England. Another Bell, at Stilton in Cambridgeshire, earned fame by selling a distinctive cheese made in Melton Mowbray to travellers on the road; in time the cheese was called after the place in which it was sold, hence Stilton. Nowadays no long-distance traffic thinks to visit the village and the Bell at Stilton, with its grandiose wrought-iron sign, faces an incongruously wide and empty village street.

Ironically, perhaps the most enduringly successful of the road's old hostelries was never an important coaching inn. The Ram Jam, between Stamford and Grantham, owes its status as one of the road's principal landmarks to a memorable name, taken from the name of a liquor brought back from India and sold there in the eighteenth century. Today, in this age of national franchises which offer little variety in the way of food and drink on our major roads, the Ram Jam is an example of how a privately owned inn can make a success of offering good food in classy surroundings.

The natural heirs of the old coaches that brought prosperity to the Great North Road's towns and villages are the forty-ton trucks that thunder up and down. When I first came to London I worked in a bookshop near Smithfield Market, by chance one of the traditional starting/finishing points of the road. One evening I shared a cup of Thermos coffee with a driver called John from Aberdeen. Three times a week he made the run from near the top of Scotland to deliver prime beef to Smithfield and of course for John the road was no such thing as the 'north' road, but the gateway south. Houseproud, he showed me round his cab: curtains, bunk beds, little stove between the seats, a television mounted on the dashboard. Hundreds if not thousands of Johns drive the road every day and night; and when the light fades, and the tachograph tells them they have reached the limit of their permitted mileage, you see them parked up in lay-bys and corralled in truckstops such as Kate's Cabin, their cabs flickering spectrally with blue light.

One of the fascinating contrasts that Jon Nicholson points up in his photographs is that between the trucker and the car driver, the old transport café and the new, all-singing, all-selling idea of the motorway service station. Unreconstructed, probably a smoker, the overalled and workbooted trucker silently

12

and contentedly fills up with his liver and bacon beneath sickly strip lighting and surrounded by utilitarian decor. The hapless car driver, by contrast, sticks fast on the flypaper that is, say, South Mimms 'service area'. Once all petrol stations looked like the one Nicholson photographed at Wooler in Northumberland: some old pumps, a tin shack, a cheery man with a rag offering to check your oil. Now they are shopping malls (the Galleria above the Hatfield Tunnel calls itself an 'Outlet Centre') selling designer leisure wear and pushing a healthy-eating agenda that favours brioches over bangers, bottled water over sweet tea.

It's this tension between old and new — what Nicholson calls the pull between reminiscence and progress — that makes the A1 such an interesting road. In the United States, Congress approved a preservation law which provides some $6 million a year to save and maintain important landmarks along Route 66. There's no such protection for the A1's layers of history. Perhaps, when those layers have finally been stripped away, people will become aware of what's been lost; and the images in this book will constitute a record of a vanished era. Meanwhile enjoy them for what they are: a tribute to a fascinating slice of British life.

St Paul's Cathedral, London EC4

We're off, and my very first glimpse of the route north is from the top of the dome of St Paul's — distances from London may be measured to Charing Cross, but the A1 starts here, right across the road.

St Paul's Cathedral, London EC4

St Paul's Cathedral, London EC4

St Paul's Cathedral, London EC4

The cathedral is a symbol of national hope and pride
— after all, it survived the Blitz, and some of our
greatest heroes are buried here — so why can't
people show its front door a bit more respect?

St Paul's Cathedral, London EC4

St Paul's Cathedral, London EC4

21

The first of many signs north. In the days of horse-drawn stage coaches, the Angel Hotel at Islington was the nearest staging post to London on the Great North Road, and even though it doesn't exist any more, its name has for some reason stuck.

Angel (A 1)
Barbican
Shoreditch
Aldgate
Bank

Except buses
taxis and
for access

Paternoster Square, London EC4

The Barbican, London EC2

Smithfield Market, London EC1

Smithfield Market, London EC1

I couldn't work out what all these tourists were doing — until I saw the plaque. I'm headed for Scotland — unlike William Wallace, whose last visit to London was a one-way trip, ending with his execution.

TO THE IMMORTAL MEMORY OF
SIR WILLIAM WALLACE

SCOTTISH PATRIOT BORN AT ELDERSLIE
RENFREWSHIRE CIRCA 1270 A.D. WHO FROM
THE YEAR 1296 FOUGHT DAUNTLESSLY
IN DEFENCE OF HIS COUNTRY'S LIBERTY AND
INDEPENDENCE IN THE FACE OF FEARFUL
ODDS AND GREAT HARDSHIP BEING
EVENTUALLY BETRAYED AND CAPTURED
BROUGHT TO LONDON AND PUT TO DEATH
NEAR THIS SPOT ON THE
23RD. AUGUST 1305

HIS EXAMPLE HEROISM AND DEVOTION
INSPIRED THOSE WHO CAME AFTER HIM
TO WIN VICTORY FROM DEFEAT AND HIS
MEMORY REMAINS FOR ALL TIME A SOURCE
OF PRIDE HONOUR AND INSPIRATION
TO HIS COUNTRYMEN

DICO TIBI VERUM LIBERTAS OPTIMA RERUM
NUNQUAM SERVILI SUB NEXU VIVITO FILI

BAS AGUS BUAIDH

St Bartholomew's Hospital, London EC1

St Bartholomew's Hospital, London EC1

Off Upper Street, London N1

Upper Street, N1   Upper Street, N1   Holloway Road, N7   Holloway Road, N7

Holloway Road, N7   Holloway Road, N19   Archway Road, N19   Archway Road, N6

HOLLOWAY
ROAD

Holloway Road, London N7

Aylmer Road, London N2

Falloden Way, London NW11

A1/A406 (North Circular Road) junction, London N3

A1/A406 (North Circular Road) junction, London NW11

There goes another fiver! If I hit too many traffic lights at red, this is going to be an expensive trip — don't these people know what windscreen wipers are for?

A1/A406 (North Circular Road) junction, London NW11

South Mimms services, Herts.

South Mimms services, Herts.

South Mimms services, Herts.

South Mimms services, Herts.

South Mimms services, Herts.

South Mimms services, Herts.

South Mimms services, Herts.

The Galleria, Hatfield, Herts.

The A1 has come a long way since the Romans marched
up it — the Hatfield Tunnel now channels six lanes
of motorway under the Galleria, a flashy shopping
mall, bypassing rural England and leaving old places
like the Comet Hotel to stand the test of time.

The Jarvis Comet Hotel, Hatfield, Herts.

Hatfield, Herts.

Near Stevenage, Herts.

Near Stevenage, Herts.

On May Day I got up at the crack of dawn to watch these
morris dancers perform their ancient ritual...

Ickwell Green, Beds'.

Ickwell Green, Beds.

...and couldn't believe my eyes when I saw that a couple of hundred other people had had the same idea. May Day is all about the fertility of spring and is one of the few pagan festivals left in this country.

Ickwell Green, Beds.

The Cross, Beeston, Beds.

Chawston, Beds.

Tempsford, Beds.

LINDEN TREE
PRESENTED
ON BEHALF OF THE
CZECH RESISTANCE
1989

During the Second World War, RAF spyplanes
took off at night from Tempsford to deliver
Czech and Free French resistance fighters
by parachute deep into occupied territory.
Their memory lives on.

Tempsford, Beds.

Tempsford, Beds.

Alconbury truckstop, Cambs.

Alconbury truckstop, Cambs.

Alconbury truckstop, Cambs.

Alconbury, Cambs.

Alconbury, Cambs.

To LONDON 64 Miles
through Huntingdon
Royston & Ware
To Huntingdon 3 Miles
To LONDON 72 Miles
through Cambridge
To Cambridge 21 Miles

Near Alconbury, Cambs.

Near Alconbury, Cambs.

Near Peterborough, Cambs.

Ribbons of light trail behind night drivers — this is a road that never sleeps, even if the occasional driver does — twenty-four hours a day, seven days a week, there's no end to the traffic.

All the truckers know Kate's Cabin — with a full breakfast like theirs under your belt, you can't go far wrong. But places like this are under threat from modern slip-road service stations — please, take a break here, support this café before it's too late.

Kate's Cabin, Chesterton, Cambs.

Kate's Cabin, Chesterton, Cambs.

Kate's Cabin, Chesterton, Cambs.

Kate's Cabin, Chesterton, Cambs.

OK Diner, near Wittering, Cambs.

Near Stamford, Lincs.

Near Grantham, Lincs.

Near Grantham, Lincs.

Near A1/M18 junction, S. Yorks.

Ferrybridge, W. Yorks.

Near Catterick, N. Yorks.

Terry and Annis Moderate have been cutting hair in Framwellgate Moor for twenty-five years since moving here from Newcastle. When they arrived, Pity Me was a separate place, but now the road between the two is a near-continuous run of buildings and the villages have almost merged into one.

Pity Me, Co. Durham

Annis's, Framwellgate Moor, Co. Durham

Washington services, Tyne & Wear

Washington services, Tyne & Wear

Washington services, Tyne & Wear

Washington services, Tyne & Wear

Washington services, Tyne & Wear

Washington services, Tyne & Wear

Welcome to Gateshead... The Angel of the North is, believe it or not, taller than a five-storey building, with wings almost as wide as a jumbo jet's. Rather like a tree, its roots are as deep as it is high, with piles twenty-two metres down anchoring it to the bedrock.

Gateshead, Tyne & Wear

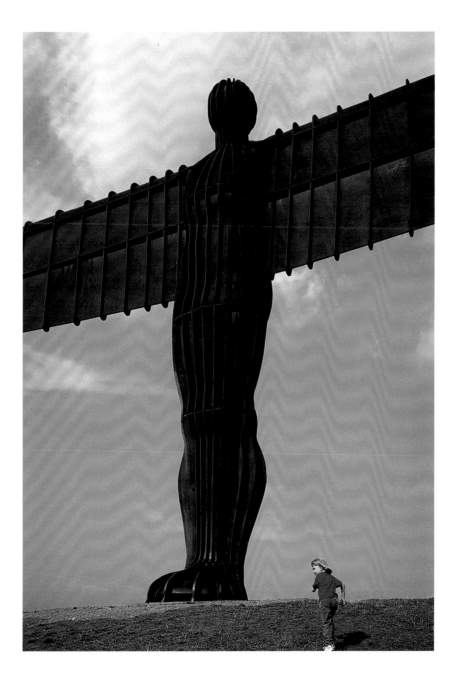

The Quayside, Newcastle upon Tyne

The Quayside, Newcastle upon Tyne

Some parts of Tyneside have done well in the recent boom. The yuppie bars springing up around Newcastle's Quayside seem a world away from the terraces and cranes further east on the docks at Wallsend.

Wallsend, Tyne & Wear

Denton Burn, Tyne & Wear

Denton Burn, Tyne & Wear

Near Hazlerigg, Tyne & Wear

I'd better get past this monster while there's still
some dual carriageway left...

Near Morpeth, Northumberland

Near Morpeth, Northumberland

Ellington, Northumberland

Alnwick, Northumberland

Alnwick, Northumberland

I made a point of catching the Shrove Tuesday pancake race at Alnwick. It's a bizarre custom that apparently dates from medieval days when women would use up leftover cooking fat (not allowed during Lent) to bake pancakes on Shrove Tuesday.

The Shrove Tuesday football match between St Paul's and St Michael's parishes. The Duke of Northumberland drops the ball from the battlements beforehand — afterwards the players jump in the river to cool off.

Alnwick Castle, Northumberland

Near Whittingham, Northumberland

Near Whittingham, Northumberland

Near Wooler, Northumberland

In the old days, stage coaches often used to cross the fields to avoid the ruts and bogs in the road. Now it's the other way round, but I thought I'd have some fun by leaving the tarmac and searching out the old A1. The driver of another four-wheel-drive vehicle kindly offered to come with me 'in case I got stuck', but didn't need to hang around — this car can do the job!

Near West Horton, Northumberland

Holy Island, Northumberland

Holy Island is cut off from the mainland for about five hours every day — its three-mile causeway is lined with barnacle-encrusted marker poles. Having checked the tide tables I thought I'd avoid delays, but I still ended up having to wait while the police removed an old bomb from the sand.

Holy Island, Northumberland

Holy Island, Northumberland

Near Ancroft, Northumberland

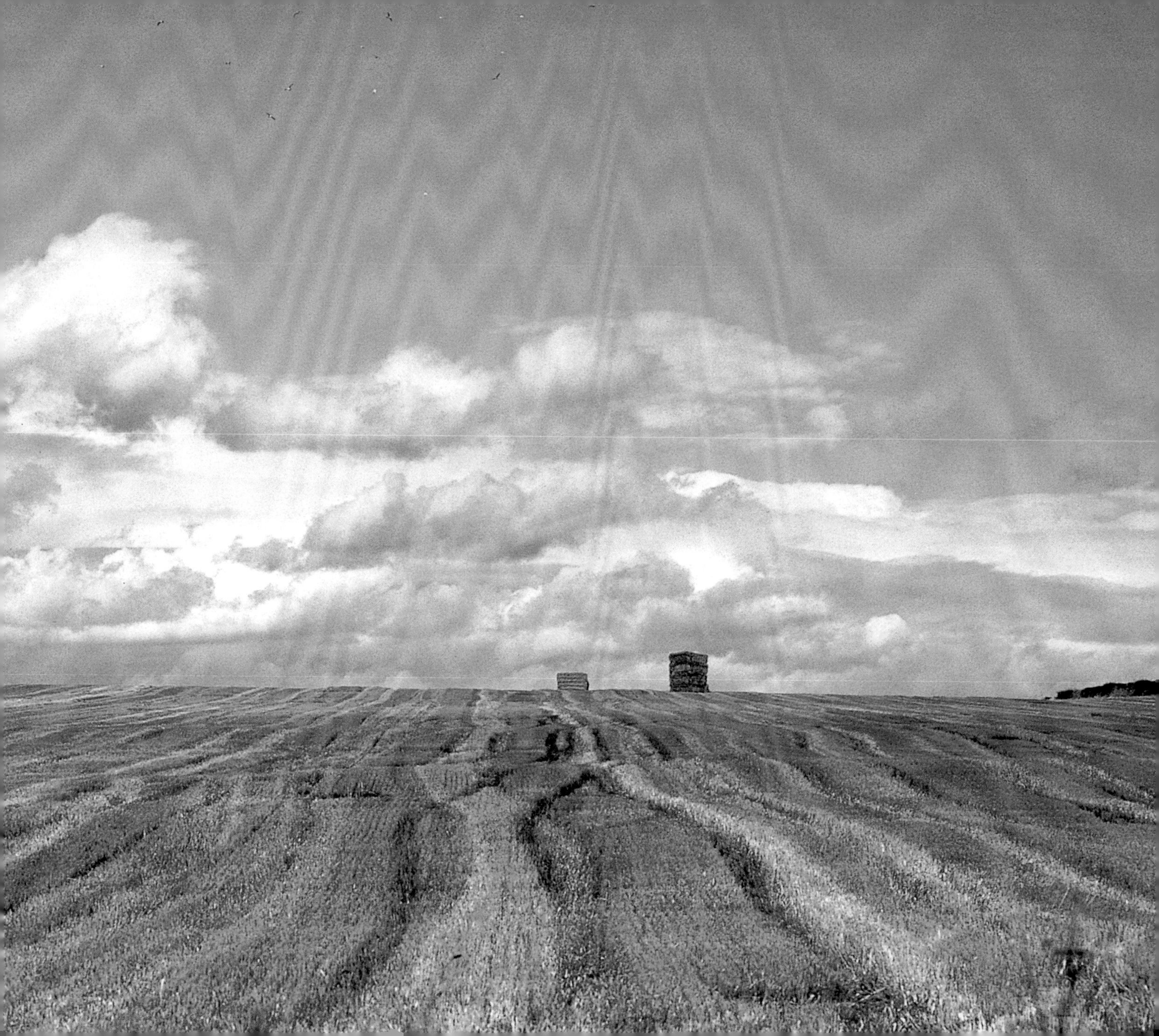

Berwick upon Tweed, Northumberland

Berwick upon Tweed, Northumberland

Berwick is a weird, in-between sort of place — not quite English and not quite Scottish, with a dialect to match. It was once a great Scottish port, and it changed hands fourteen times before finally becoming part of England.

Berwick upon Tweed, Northumberland

Berwick upon Tweed, Northumberland

Berwick upon Tweed, Northumberland

Berwick upon Tweed, Northumberland

Berwick upon Tweed, Northumberland

Berwick upon Tweed, Northumberland

Near Lamberton, Borders

Near Lamberton, Borders

Scotland at last — and the last house in England,
seen from the north bank of the Tweed.

River Tweed, looking towards Horncliffe, Northumberland

Near Chirnside, Borders

Near Chirnside, Borders

Near Burnmouth, Borders

Burnmouth, Borders

St Abbs, Borders

Pease Bay caravan park, Borders

Near Cockburnspath, Borders

Near Dunbar, East Lothian

The landfill site near Dunbar is a place probably best left to the seagulls to do what they do best.

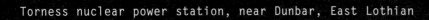

Torness nuclear power station, near Dunbar, East Lothian

Dunbar, East Lothian

Near Haddington, East Lothian

As I pulled into Edinburgh a cloud of smoke hovered over the city. Arthur's Seat was once a volcano — perhaps it was erupting — but on closer inspection the smoke turned out to be a heather fire.

Arthur's Seat, Edinburgh

Calton Hill, Edinburgh

You get one of the best views of Edinburgh from Calton Hill, all the way along Princes Street. What a great place.

Princes Street, Edinburgh

Waverley Market, Edinburgh

Princes Street, Edinburgh

Princes Street, Edinburgh

National Gallery of Scotland, Edinburgh

Princes Street Gardens, Edinburgh

Edinburgh Castle

Calton Hill, Edinburgh

Calton Hill is known as the 'Acropolis of the north', and here you can see why. Anyway, this is the end of the road — or the start, depending on your point of view. Time to turn around now and head for home.

the car in front is a
TOYOTA

I would like to thank all at
Olympus Optical; Metro Imaging;
Clare Bruce at Kodak Professional.
And, of course, Toyota — you're
not having the car back.

First published in 2000 by
HarperCollins*Illustrated*,
an imprint of
HarperCollins*Publishers*
77—85 Fulham Palace Road
London W6 8JB

The HarperCollins website address is:
www.fireandwater.com

Photographs and captions © 2000 Jon Nicholson
Introduction © 2000 Nigel Richardson

Jon Nicholson hereby asserts his moral rights to
be identified as the author of this Work.

A CIP catalogue record for this book is available
from the British Library.

ISBN: 0 00 220199 2

04 03 02 01 00

9 8 7 6 5 4 3 2 1

Colour separation by Colourscan, Singapore
Printed and bound by The Bath Press, UK